CRUZ CONTROL

YOUR FAST TRACK TO A SUCCESSFUL REAL ESTATE CAREER

MELISSA CRUZ

ISBN: 978-1-966798-59-0

I dedicate this book to:

My children Arielle and Darius. You both push me to be the best version of me. I love you so much.

To my hubby Larry. Thank you for your constant support. I couldn't do this without you.

To my mom and dad who love me unconditionally and cheer me on with everything I set out to do.

To my dear sister and guardian angel. Thank you for teaching me how to reach for the stars and live life to the fullest. I miss you everyday.

To all of the mentors I have had in my life. You showed this girl that she can truly achieve what she sets out to do because of how much you believe in me.

Welcome to *Cruz Control*—Your No-BS, Step-by-Step Guide to Real Estate Success!

Think passing the real estate exam was the hard part? Think again. The real challenge starts *now*—figuring out how to actually build a business that doesn't leave you broke, burned out, or questioning your life choices.

That's where this book comes in.

Whether you're freshly licensed and feeling like a deer in headlights or you've been winging it for a while and need a serious game plan, *Cruz Control* is your **fast track to success**.

Real estate coach, industry leader, and all-around business *fixer* **Melissa Cruz** dishes out everything they *didn't* teach you in real estate school—like how to find clients without feeling like a pushy salesperson, build relationships that actually turn into deals, and create a business that works *for you* (not the other way around).

Inside, you'll find:

- Real talk about what works (and what's a total waste of time)
- Actionable strategies that you can use *today*—not "someday"
- Space to map out your own path, so you're not just reading, you're *doing*
- Personal stories that prove you're not alone in the chaos
- Motivation to keep going—because let's be honest, you'll need it

Cruz Control isn't just a book—it's your **business GPS**. No more guessing. No more "What the heck do I do now?" moments. Just a clear, proven roadmap to help you build a business that feels *good* and actually *makes money*.

No fluff. No gimmicks. Just real, practical strategies to help you win in real estate—your way.

Let's get you in *Cruz Control*—because success shouldn't feel like an uphill battle.

Table of Contents

PART ONE

Life is a matter of choices, and every choice you make makes you.

—John C. Maxwell

So Glad You're Here

Let me start off by saying congratulations to you, friend. By purchasing this book, you have made a decision, no matter where you are in your business, that you are meant for more. You have just taken a stance for you, for your family, and for your business. Way to go!! I could not be more proud of you. Please know now that this journey you have decided to embark on is going to be a marathon. There is no magic pill or get rich quick scheme. If you are looking to build a long lasting career in real estate, it is going to take hard work, dedication, commitment, some luck, and a little faith. There will be days when you are going to want to give up. Please don't. Please pull this book out and let it remind you that you *can* do this. Your mistakes and failures do not determine your success. To get from where you are now to where you want to be will require some falls, cuts, and bruises along the way.

Before we get too far, let's get to some honest truth. If you are anything like me, you went to real estate school, you passed your class, your exams, and left the testing center just as confused as you were before starting the class in the first place. Right!?! I never came down so fast from any sort of excitement before. Don't get me wrong, the information we learn in real estate school is absolutely necessary and helpful but it's not the only piece to this puzzle. It's really the start piece you put on your gameboard. This is where having a roadmap aka a business plan, can help you gain clarity on what you need to do to find success in your own special way. Once you become licensed there will be a lot of people sharing with you their advice on how you should go about building your business. While that is really nice and can be sometimes helpful, try to take it in and park it. You are going to be discovering yourself so much in the beginning and everyone builds their business differently. It is easier to work on your plan when you can focus on you.

The Importance of Creating a Business Plan

I cannot express enough how important it is to have a plan. Not just a dream but a written series of steps on how you will achieve such a dream. For most of us that get into the business, we have never written a business plan before. If this is you, then you are in the right place. Heck, even if you have written a plan and it's not working, you are still in the right place. Maybe you wrote a plan because someone said you should, but you don't actually use it. I cannot tell you how many agents I meet write a plan and then toss it in a folder only to never look at it again. Together, we are going to dive deep into how to build a plan that is right for you. I would also recommend you take this plan you create and go over it with your broker. They care so much about your success and this could help them help you stay accountable to what truly matters. If you need more support or clarity, you can always take a class online or in person. These types of classes are offered often. Now, allow me to share with you a story on why I am going hard about this.

My First "Plan"

I got into real estate in June of 2016 and I joined a local brokerage in town. One of the first things I was asked to do was what I am asking you to do, write a business plan. My initial reaction was, how the heck am I going to do that? I don't know anything yet. As you can probably imagine I questioned it big time. I did eventually come around and accepted help on creating my very first business plan. It was really weird and if I am being honest I wasn't one hundred percent sure if what I created was in fact going to work. Nevertheless, I made a commitment to completing it.

I carried that business plan with me everywhere. At that time, the brokerage I worked for offered us something called "floor duty." It consists of spending a few hours at work in a dedicated office up front, where any leads that called or walked in went to the person in that position. I committed to working floor duty as much as I could each month. I would also take as many leads as other agents were willing to give. I held open houses at least twice a month and I joined a women's networking group that met once a week. At the end of each quarter I would go back and see how many shifts I worked, how many open houses I held, and how many meetings I went to. By the end of my first year, I was able to see exactly how I spent that time and where my business was coming from. I didn't have much that first year, but I did have enough business that allowed me to reflect upon it. Having that plan helped me more than I ever thought it would.

Moral of the story: write the darn plan; your future business will thank you for it.

Mission, Value, and Transferable Skills

I know you are excited to dive into creating this business plan, but there are a few things you may want to consider tackling first. For starters, spend some time discovering your *why*. Why did you get into real estate? What are you hoping this business will help you accomplish? Is there a specific problem you are hoping to solve? Did you yourself have a bad experience when you purchased or sold a home? Or maybe you had a good experience? Those are just a few questions to jumpstart your mind.

Take some time with this. Try and push past the superficial "freedom" related answers you might think of. Allow yourself the space to be honest with what it is you really want with no judgment. Paint a picture of what you'd want if you were to achieve everything you imagined. This is what we call "The Best Case" scenario. Your *why*, when you finally get to the core, should make you feel something inside. That's how you know you hit something big.

Once you know why you are here, how will you share that with the world? How will you share the mission you are on? Not only for the people you hope to do business with but your family too. This could lead you into creating a "Mission Statement." From that mission statement, you can create your "Twenty Second Elevator Pitch." That will be a really great way to let people know why they should hire you to help them buy or sell. It shows them that you aren't just here to make money, or shove real estate down their throat but to help *them* achieve *their* goals.

I want you to understand something right now about our industry: we matter. Not only for the obvious value we bring to a transaction, but so much more. Our role, although small, is a really big deal. We have the opportunity to change peoples lives in the most beautiful way. I believe to my core that what we get to help people accomplish today will in fact leave a positive ripple effect for years to come. When you can change your mindset to think about the impact you have, it makes how you show up at work even better. It makes the hard days of building a business just a little bit easier because this is so much bigger than us.

The next thing I want you to think about are your values. A little later on you are going to be working on an exercise to find your ideal client, but for now let's focus on you. What is it that you value? What is important to you? Why are those things important to you? What do you enjoy? What you don't enjoy? What do you stand for? If it's been a long time or you've never sat down to ask yourself these questions, take your time with them. Don't just take what first comes to mind at face value.

Really dig deep on who you are and what matters to you most, both internally and externally. Trust me, by taking the time to do this now, it will make it a lot easier to say "No" to the wrong people later.

The last thing we need to cover are your transferable skills. "What skills?" you may ask. Well, the ones you bring with you, silly. For some reason when people get into the business they somehow forget that they were great at something once upon a time. For many people real estate is a second career, and I find that when agents can go back and reflect on what skills they've acquired in their lifetime, it really helps them a lot in this business. Not only does it bring a level of confidence, but it also shows what value you bring that many others don't have. Be proud of that and find a way to continue using those skills.

Here are a few questions to help you remember why you are so awesome already.

- What did you do before you got into real estate?
- What do/did people always go to you for?
- How can you incorporate those skills into your real estate business?

The Time I Went Against What I Valued

If you don't believe me just yet, let me tell you another story. One Saturday I was working at an open house in a condominium complex. Then, this lady approached and I of course welcomed her in. She quickly shared that she wasn't looking to buy a condo but instead needed help selling one. She wanted to sell her condo and purchase a single family home. She mentioned coming into the open house because she saw all of my signs. Exciting right!?! I followed up with her after the open house and scheduled a listing appointment/buyer appointment. I was really nervous but also very excited. I was about to have my first "twofer" deal. I met with her and her husband and locked everything in. At first everything seemed to be fine. She has done this a time or two before, so she didn't have a buttload of questions. That made things feel smooth. Then as soon as we went live on her home she started to show her crazy. The calls and messages from her were relentless. She was very stubborn and didn't care about anyone else. She just wanted what she wanted. It was quickly becoming very difficult to please her. I couldn't get her to reason. She made it difficult every step of the way. I cried more times than I can count. And to make it worse as we were nearing closing on the two properties, she called me to say she couldn't close. That she was sorry and she would not be closing is what she said. The reason she gave was ridiculous and absolutely not a valid reason not to close. After crying yet again on the floor at the office, I finally got her to calm down and close when we were intending to. We closed on a Friday and boy I was so happy. That night I picked up dinner for my family to celebrate. The very next day, I was so sick. I couldn't get out of bed. It was as if everything I had been holding onto just by myself came crashing down.

At first I was pissed at her. Then, as I lay there in bed with just my thoughts I realized that I should have never been her agent in the first place. She taught me a very valuable lesson: I needed to slow down. Which, if you know me, is not in my vocabulary. As funny as that is, this was no funny matter. I could not afford to live this again and again with each person I worked with. I had to learn how to make sure that the person I worked with had similar values as me. As I got better, I started to reflect on what the heck happened. There were indeed red flags all along, but I chose to ignore them. I spent the entire next week working on building my value proposition. I share this with you because I want you to know that you deserve to work with the right people. It isn't worth it going against who you are and what you ultimately deserve from the people you serve. I get that this business will require sacrifice from time to time. I'm just saying not sticking to your values shouldn't be one of them.

Overview of Books Purpose - Clarity and Intention

The main purpose of this book is to help you create a simplified, specific yet action-packed plan to help you achieve your goals in real estate. For some of you, this might be a financial goal. For others, this could be a unit or volume type of goal. Whatever it is, I found the best way I was able to create my yearly plan was to first dream far out into the future. By doing this, I allowed myself the space to paint a picture of what could be if I reached my goals. The approach I had was a glass half full type of mentality. "What if everything did work out?" was what I asked myself. By going to the future, I was able to work my way backwards to where I was right then. I set goals as far out as ten years. I will then work towards five years, three years, and then lastly on the current year. This brought me so much clarity and made me more motivated for my journey. It made me deeply rooted in why I was here, and the power that showing up *today* had on *tomorrow*. If you have never done this before, I highly recommend you spend some time dreaming a little bit about how things can really work out for you. Dream with no judgment or fear. Let that childlike imagination come out to play again.

All that to say, by doing this exercise now, you will have no other way to live than on purpose. The purpose of this book is to help with your real estate business but what I think you'll find is this will help you on an internal level as well. You see, I am a firm believer that we are our business. While we may technically help people buy *houses,* our role is so much bigger. Don't forget it.

Overview of Books Structure

This book is designed to take you step by step into creating a plan that is the best version of you. The first part includes a breakdown of the elements for a good business plan. This will include pieces around your strengths, time, and what you will be tracking. Then we will discuss how this shows up in your life and when you will implement these activities. Lastly, we will uncover what specific pieces of your business you will be tracking. Once these are completed then we will take a deep dive into the right lead generation for you.

In the second part, we will learn about the work/life balance of this job and what it means for you. I will share some studies around this topic to help guide you on setting the proper expectations for yourself.

That last part will recap everything we discussed and learned. I am going to encourage you along the way to make decisions. Not only making them but also committing to them. There are highlights, additional resources, and links in the back of this book for you as well.

The Goal

By the time you get to the end of this book, you will have completed your plan for next year or at least the end of this year, depending on when you are reading this. There will be several times throughout the book when I will be asking you to stop and complete that section. It is imperative that you take your time with this. The whole point is to help you finish so you don't have to guess what you should be doing everyday. Not a day should go by where you wake up and then have to think of what to do. Having a plan helps you take the guesswork out of what you are doing and why you are doing it. There is something so grounding in that; it seeps into my core. Also, it doesn't help you to gather all of the information and then do nothing with it.

If I may, here I will share a goal of mine I have for you: I want this book to be your guiding light. I want this book to be one that you go back to time and time again. Not just for business but when you feel lost in life and need some help with direction. Can you tell I am a girl full of hope?

Where It All Began

Before you continue, I want to share one more story about the birth of this, at first, template. Back in 2019 I switched over to a new brokerage. A few months after joining, I decided I wanted to become a mentor. I was finding success in my business and I wanted to help other agents do the same. There was one small problem: I wasn't quite sure how. All the same, I didn't spend too much time stressing about it because I figured I would learn once I had a mentee. Then, the first one came, and then the second one. They came pretty fast, and at that time I obviously didn't have a polished plan or anything for them. I was sorta reacting to whatever it was they needed.

You know what happened next? Covid. Freaking Covid. Not only was I in the middle of finding my way to helping my mentees, I was also still working my own real estate business. When the pandemic happened, I started to panic just as the rest of the world. In an instant, my life changed and all of these questions started running through my mind. How in the world was I going to sell real estate? How was I going to earn money? Just like that, I went from a full time working real estate professional to full time mom and elementary teacher for my two children. Insert "breath, girl, breathe." Side note, anyone else talk to themselves?

One afternoon, I sat down and took a look at what was on my plate. Even though I had no idea how long we were going to be locked down, I still needed to figure out what I was going to do. That's when it hit me—my mentees. If I didn't have the time and capabilities to "be" an agent, then I was going to pour everything I had into them. I remember feeling like, "aha! I got it!"

It was then I started to look at my time and started to create a plan. Here is what I knew:

1. I had to teach from 9-5 Monday through Friday
2. I could put in 4 hours each day into real estate Monday through Friday
3. I had Saturday and Sunday to create a training program; and meal prep for the week

Knowing this, I was able to time block and create very specific activities I needed to follow in order for me to make it. The first thing I did was set a day and time that my mentees and I met virtually to discuss our week. Then, I wrote a business plan template that every single mentee had to complete. They could not start any other training with me until this piece was done. What you will be completing throughout this book is an updated version of such plan. I have further tweaked it, the more experience I gained in the field, on top of other things I have learned along the way.

Ok, so there you have it. Hopefully, by now you understand the importance of having a written plan for how you are going to show up for your business every day. I have beaten this up enough. Let's jump into the elements of a good business plan.

PART TWO

Courage doesn't always roar. Sometimes courage is the quiet voice at the end of the day saying, 'I will try again tomorrow.'

—Mary Anne Radmacher

Crafting Your Business Plan

As we work though building our plans, let's first discuss what elements make up a great business plan. Have you ever heard of S.M.A.R.T. goals? Did you know that George Doran, Arthur Miller, and James Cunningham developed that in 1981? How cool is it that it's still relevant today? If you haven't heard of it, here is a breakdown below explaining what each letter means.

Specific: When you are thinking about what you need to do to hit your goals, you want to make them as specific as possible. Nail it down to the actual "thing" you will do.

Measurable: It is important that what you choose to do is something that can be measured. Over time this is going to give you data about you and how you are showing up for your business. It will show you what is working and what isn't working.

Attainable: I know earlier I talked about vision casting and that is great and all, but this is not the time to set unrealistic goals that you know will not be achieved in a year's time. I am not saying to play small or anything. I am saying to give yourself the opportunity to grow and stretch in a healthy way. Building a business is already hard enough, and you don't need to add any additional stress in your life.

Realistic: To go along with the previous element, make sure to be honest and real with yourself. At this stage in your life you are who you are. Do we grow and evolve? Yes, but please don't try to be someone you are not. Whatever it is you choose, make sure it aligns with who you are. Unless you are truly ready to commit to actual change, be realistic with your approach.

Timely: Last but not least, time. Putting a timestamp on your goals can help you create healthy milestones along the way. As I have mentioned before, when you are done with this book you will have created a plan for the next year. I want to encourage you to also do the same with your life's goals three, five, and ten years down the road. Although this isn't a perfect science and some things change, it is your best way to stay on task with what means the most to you.

Keep these elements in mind as you start to make decisions about your lead generation activities. Make sure that each one of these shows up for each strategy you will build a plan around. Don't worry if you aren't sure about what strategies to pick yet—we will uncover that together.

The Right Lead Generation for You

One of the biggest lessons I learned over the years about lead generating for real estate business was to stay true to who I am. I remember when I began I kept being told there were certain ways to build this business. It had to be this way or that way, but none of them really felt organic to me. It didn't help that I didn't know what the hell I was doing. I was just taking in everything that was coming to me. What I shared earlier about my first business plan was what I did when I first started. As time went on, I learned that I really loved face to face interactions.

I may not have had a ton of confidence, but when I was able to get belly to belly with someone, I got more "yes's" than "no's." This awareness opened my eyes to start looking into all the possibilities I had around me. From that moment on I began looking at what I was doing, and if that effort was in fact bringing me business. I think it's important to share this with you because I want you to give yourself permission to be you. The more authentic you can be, the better you and your business will be.

Another massive thing I learned too around 2020 was, I am not a mother or a business owner, or a spouse. I am all of those things, everyday. When I was lead generating how someone else thought I should, I felt like three different people. I was miserable and pretty damn exhausted, both physically and mentally. When the world shut down, I couldn't take it anymore. The right way to lead generate and build a business was to be one person: me. I am a mom *and* a business owner *and* a spouse, not or. That right there was a game changer for me. Who are you?

Think about what you have going on in your life right now. What makes you happy? Do you have any hobbies or hidden talents? Do you maybe work another job? Are you from where you live? What if you aren't? Are you an introvert? Are you an extrovert?

I know it's a lot of questions, but don't be afraid to go there with yourself. All of them will help you narrow down what your approach could be. It is also going to help you stay true to yourself. If this is a challenge for you and you're not sure where is best to start, then maybe you should try some common ways. It may help to try a few approaches so you can learn what feels good and where you are actually getting results from.

Since starting my career, I have found that this journey has been somewhat of a self-discovery journey. I have learned new things about myself. I have overcome challenges I didn't always think I had in me. I have had dreams awaken that I had long forgotten about. It has been really fun. Don't forget to enjoy that for you too.

Implementation

Once you have sat down and come up with your plan, the next thing that needs to be done is finding the time and space everyday to implement what you said you were going to do. I read a book years ago called "The 12 Week Year." That book changed the way I looked at any given year. It also showed me how I needed to show up in order to stay consistent with my activities. The biggest thing the book taught me was slowing down. Ugh, yes, slowing down. You know that I do not move at that speed. So as you can imagine, that took a lot of effort and focus. I knew, though. that if I wanted to grow I needed to listen to the people ahead of me and find a way.

The challenge for you is going to be to figure out how you best operate. Are you a morning person? Are you a night person? When do you have the best energy? Are you a time blocker? Are you a checklist person? What do you do to prepare your mind for flow time? Focus time? How do you prepare yourself for success and get rid of distractions?

Again, lots of questions to answer, but I promise that if you can answer those questions as true to you as you can, you will absolutely find the right way for you. I might add that if you are going to spend all this time getting into this business, finding ways to lead generate for business and you are going against who you are, you won't last long. You will either be that 24/7 agent and burn yourself out or you will continue to spin in circles trying everything only to realize nothing is working and you quit. I don't want that for you. You shouldn't want that for you. I truly believe that if you are someone who wants to be here and find a way to be successful and achieve all of your dreams and goals, you can! It takes intention, time, and effort. Also, a lot of mindset convos too. More on that later.

So where do you start? As I have mentioned earlier, start big and work backwards. Take the big numbers you need to hit by the end of the year and back track your way to how many of each thing needs to be accomplished each week in order to achieve the big goal. Let me make something very clear before I move on. What I am referencing here is NOT results. I am talking about the actual, specific activities you need to do every day you are working your real estate business. Those things are in your control. You can't control results.

Back to the 12 Week Year. In the book, the authors teach its readers how to view the year in quarters. It stemmed from looking at people in sales and their behavior when Q4 came around every year. For some people, when the last quarter of the year comes around all of a sudden they remember they had certain goals to hit in order to achieve, fill in the blank. Oddly enough some of them do end up hitting their goals. What the authors share is, what if you had that mentality all year long. What if each quarter was your year? Each week was your month? Interesting right? They also teach their readers about the leading and lagging measures of our businesses. What's the difference? The leading measures are the daily specific dollar producing activities that one must do to keep the needle moving in their business. The lagging measures are the results of such activities.

While lagging measures are important and necessary to make income, it isn't what you'll want to focus on or track. If you are not getting results, it will stem from the activities you are doing or not doing that can change that. If you are getting results you can still go back and look at what you've done that got you the results in the first place. The point here is your daily conversations and activities matter most. Get that right and the rest will come through.

Tracking for Your Business

I do want to talk a little bit here about tracking for your business. Later on in the book you will have clearer direction on this, but I thought we should already start thinking about this aspect of our business. Now as far as what you'll be tracking, here it is:

- Daily, weekly, monthly, quarterly, and yearly activities
- Your finances around your business. What comes in and what goes out.
- Returns on your investments like your time and money

That may seem like a lot to you, but if you make time to focus on each of these, it won't be as overwhelming. It's crucial to keep a pulse on these though. You do not want to wake up at the end of the year or when you're doing your taxes to learn that you should have pivoted a long time ago. As we get more into the specifics of your plan, together we will create a list of what you need to track.

Let's Get to It

The anticipation is over. Let's jump on creating our plans! When I am helping agents create their business plans, I like to help them learn that less is more. Because when you get through the weeds of finding yourself and finding what works best for you, you want to keep your efforts simple.

Trust me, building a business and finding success isn't always doing new things. It's finding what works and doing that *every single damn day*. Over time it may get mundane and boring, but that is what building a successful business looks like. Could you spice things up a little?

Absolutely. Just give time to that which you are going to commit to. If you change your activities/message often, it will confuse your audience.

Speaking of which, who are you going to target? How do you know when you have met your ideal client? How do you ask for the business? What problem do you solve for these people? Again, lots of questions, but they will bring you so much clarity. This is also another reason why, when you commit to a strategy, you benefit more from sticking with it for a while. Too much change too fast can cause more confusion than you intended. We will definitely dig deeper on that in a bit.

Your Sphere of Influence aka SOI

Let's start by defining what a sphere is and who they are. A sphere is someone who knows you, likes you, and trusts you already. They are not acquaintances or strangers. Who makes up this category? That's an awesome question. The people that make up this category are your family, your friends, your past clients, your colleagues you work with at a W2 job, and your vendor partners. You could also add people here who you might go to church with, or who share similar hobbies/interests with you.

What happens if you are new to the town you live in? Do you still think you have a sphere? Absolutely! If you know people in other areas and states you can still place referrals and collect a referral fee for it. It is a great way to build some other income in real estate too. If you meet other agents and create genuine relationships, they could be considered a sphere too. You may not have to "touch" them that often but you still need a systematic approach to staying top of mind with them as well.

If you are a new(er) agent, you will probably spend a good chunk of time in the beginning letting this specific group of people know you are in real estate. That's a great place to start. Keep in mind as a new agent, you will not have any data to refer back to. So for you, tracking everything your first year is really going to help set a baseline for you in the coming years.

If you are not new and you already have closings and data of your own stats, then that's wonderful. You are going to pull those out and learn what story it's telling you. How much of your business came from your sphere? Is it what you were shooting for? Do you want more this year? What were your best quarters of the year? Meaning, what quarter did your closings happen in? If you are looking to get more business, then you may want to spend some time creating intentional opportunities for you. By planning and using technology you can have this smooth sailing.

Once you have identified your sphere and answered all of the questions, if they applied, now what? What needs to happen in order for you to stay top of mind with this group? Easy—sorta. In this day and age there are so many ways that we can communicate. My suggestion would be to have a plan for several of these communication types. For example:

- Phone Call
- Text/Video text
- Email
- Social Media
- Pop-bys
- Events
- Handwritten Cards

The idea is to incorporate several of these touches throughout the year. You want to be top of mind whenever they need something. Not that you need to be all things to all people but I bet you know people that they could need. If not, that might be another thing you could work on.

Speaking of, when we look at our vendor partners we should be applying top of mind activities to them too. Consider this: are you genuinely looking to partner with them and grow each other's businesses. If so, how do you do that? How do you add value to their life? Do you just reach out to them when you need something? Is what you have now a one way relationship? Is it a partnership? It's ok if you've just realized this. What isn't ok is knowing this now and doing nothing about it, yet still expecting our partners to support us all the time. Partnerships should be a win-win for both parties in it.

Getting a full picture of what it will take to do each one before you decide on what to choose will help. Just as our lead generation, what you choose should be something that aligns with you. Let's break down some of these touches.

Phone Calls

Now, when I say phone calls I am just talking about our sphere here. We will have other calls to make with other efforts and follow up. That is not what we are doing here. Depending how big your database is, you may need to organize your approach. If you have a smaller database it's possible to call everyone once a month. Maybe every other month, if that is too much for you and them. If you have a bigger database, you can either call everyone once a quarter or focus on your top 100 people.

Example:

100 people: Once a month = 25 a week = 5 a day for 5 days a week

250 people: Over two months = 31.25 a week = 6.25 a day for 5 days a week

500 people: Once a quarter = 41 a week = 8.2 a day for 5 days a week

You might be thinking, "ok so what am I calling them about?" Again, great question. Here are a few examples to help with the "what" part of these convos.

- Thinking of You
- Invitation to an event you have coming up
- Invitation to an event happening in town you thought they might be interested in
- How is life?
- I saw you shared "fill in the blank" on Social Media
- Happy Birthday
- Happy Anniversary
- Happy House - Aversary
- Appreciation/Gratitude
- Mother's Day/Father's Day

The list is endless. You could even tap into the holidays throughout the year. Also, in case you weren't aware, we have three National months around our industry that are great conversation starters:

- April: National Fair Housing Month
- June: National Homeownership Month
- September: National Realtor Safety Month

Text/Video Text:

Similar to phone calls, never underestimate the power of a good text message. Better yet, a video message. Sometimes if you don't have time to chat with people for more than a few minutes, you can definitely plug this play in. This still gives the same effect of seeing your name and face. You can still share any of the things listed previously.

How do we get you to do this systematically and maybe at once? This is where you will want to use a CRM (Customer Relationship Management) tool. There are many out there for real estate agents that are really great. There are some that are quite simple yet effective, and then there are some that have all of the bells and whistles. Before you go blowing your budget, I suggest you take time to figure out what you can afford and what specifically you need it for. Then, see what CRM is best for you in this season of your business.

You may be tempted to immediately jump into spending top dollar for one, but honestly, if you aren't even going to use it, don't bother. I have made that mistake before and as best as my intentions were on using what they sold me with, I really hadn't. I don't know if that was good or bad but I am a simple person and I am best when I can keep things simple; it helps me stay consistent. Maybe some of you reading this right now may not have a budget yet, but that's ok too, for now. What you will want to use is either a spreadsheet or a notebook. You can grow to a place where you can afford to spend on a better system down the road.

I would like to add that there is nothing wrong with starting where you are. Oftentimes we can be our worst critics and it is easy to start judging ourselves where we feel we are lacking. This is called humble beginnings, my friend. Be proud of betting on yourself. Period.

Email:

I know, I know. You are probably thinking, "who still sends emails and actually gets business these days?" Answer: many people. Sending emails is an easy way to stay in front of people in your database. Typically, I see agents send out monthly newsletters. If you want to start email campaigns, this could be a good place to start. Like any other strategy you choose to implement before you start sending emails tomorrow, I am going to encourage you to slow down a second and create a plan. What is it you are emailing about? What outcome are you hoping for? How important is building this to you? Is it worth your time and energy? Here are some ideas of what kind of emails you can send and what they can be about:

- Monthly Market Updates
- Community Events
- Customer Appreciation Events
- Landscaping Tips
- Outdoor Decor
- Staging Tips
- Food Recipes
- Organizations You Support
- Fundraisers
- Highlight Vendor Partners
- New Restaurants
- New Parks and Schools

Monthly emails aren't the only way to go. You could also send these kinds of emails weekly:

- Renting vs Buyer Campaign
- When Selling Your Home
- Restaurant Highlights
- Motivation
- Vendor Partner Highlight

You may have heard that email marketing is dead—not true. Or that people don't open their emails—that one does have a little truth to it. Here is my take on that. If you send people things of value then they will open them. You want to update and remind people you are an agent but don't sell them to death. No one wants that. That is the quickest way to turn people off. In other words, if you have something to say, say it with purpose or don't waste your time. Be more interesting than you are interested.

Social Media:

Let me start off by saying that I realize some of you reading this may not be on social media. Or social media may be an area of opportunity for you. Either way, here are my two cents on this topic. If you aren't actively on social media right now, your clients are probably not either. Hmmm...Have you ever noticed that? On the flip side, if you are someone who is actively using social media as a "lead generation" strategy, do you or have you gotten business from there that has closed? If yes, great. If not, is that really a strategy or does it just *feel* like it because you are doing something and *feel* busy doing it? I know that sounds mean, but it's true. We are here because we are building a for profit business, aren't we? So really take some time to think about if this is an area you genuinely want to grow in. If you are choosing to focus on social media because others think you should, it might be wise to ask yourself why? It is much easier to stay committed to something to actually want to do and not what people think you should. Give it some thought. Dig deeper if you need to.

That being said, let's say that you are on social media and/or you want to grow your business using this tool. Awesome. Let's create an intentional plan so no time is wasted. Here are a few questions to consider before you start nailing down a plan.

1. What platforms are you wanting to grow?
2. Who is your ideal client?
3. What is the problem you solve for those clients?

4. How often do you plan on posting?
5. Are you willing to do videos?
6. What is your CTA (Call to Action)
7. What is your follow up system behind it?

You may find more questions coming to you when you start diving in ,but these are a good place to start. Let's take each one of these questions and share some examples.

What platform are you wanting to grow?

- Facebook
- Instagram
- YouTube
- TikTok
- Pinterest
- LinkedIn

Who is your ideal client?

- What do they do for a living?
- How much money do they make?
- Where do they shop?
- Do they own a home now or rent?
- What do they wear?
- Where do they hangout?
- Where do they dine?
- What do they drive?
- Are they indecisive?
- What do they value?
- What hobbies do they have?
- Do they have a family?

- Do they want to start a family?
- Is this their first home or second home?
- Are they downsizing because their kids are off to college?

What is the problem you solve for these clients?

- Is it first time home buyers?
- Is it people who need help downsizing?
- Are these people getting divorced?
- Are these clients elderly?
- Are these clients investors?
- What type of investor?

How often do you plan on posting?

- Once a week
- Twice a week
- Three times a week
- Everyday
- Multiple times a day

Are you willing to do videos?

- What will you shoot videos around?
- Neighborhoods
- Restaurants
- Shops
- Education
- Area history
- Interviews
- Market Updates

What is your CTA (Call to Action)?

- What is it you want people to do when they see your posts?
- What is it you want them to do with it?
- Where should they go?
- Where are they being directed?

What is your follow up system behind it?

- When people interact with you how are you going to respond?
- How will you stay top of mind?
- How will you show up intentionally?
- What does the convo look like outside of social media?
- How often will you reach out to people you have a convo with?
- When are you adding them to your database?

Ok, let's take a sec to catch our breath. I know that was a lot. I wanted to go there with you because if you planned on "just" posting and expecting business from it, it ain't happening. Everything you do for your business should be done with purpose. I suppose that is my theme here in this book.

Oh, and if you are reading this and you're like "crap this is totally me," then good too!! It's time to wake up and take action, baby.

Pop-Bys

Pop-bys are a really cute way to show up in people's lives. Depending on who and how many people you plan on doing this for, that could determine the frequency. I have seen agents do this monthly or quarterly. If you plan on doing this monthly then it might be a good idea to see if there is someone that can do these for you. The pop-bys are wonderful, don't get me wrong but it also involves putting in time. If you don't have that time that's ok, find someone who does.

Let's back up a minute. I realized I haven't even shared what that is. A pop-by is when you "pop" by someone's home with a little gift. The gift is something small. Ideally, the cost for these should be under $5 for each one. You can find some really cute ideas on Pinterest. If this is not an area of strength for you, no worries; there are companies you could pay for this as well. Doing these pop bys can give you several opportunities to reach out to each person. Here is an example:

1. At the start: "Hi, *insert their name*, it's *insert your name*. Will you be home on, *insert day*? I have a little something I want to drop off for you."

2. On the day: "Hi, *insert name*, it's *insert your name*. I am heading over to your place today to drop off my gift. Will I see you?"

3. If you saw them: "It was so nice seeing you last week. Hope you enjoyed the little gift. I really appreciate you and value our friendship."

4. If you missed them: "I am so sorry I missed you. Did you get the little gift I left for you? Hope you enjoyed it. I really appreciate you and value our friendship."

Not too shabby, huh? This could also be done via text if that is the preference here. The way you communicate isn't as important as getting it done.

Events:

If you are a newer agent reading this you, may not have the funds to put on your own events. That is ok. You can totally use your brokerage's events to start with. Or, if you spent time building some solid vendor partner relationships, they could help sponsor the event so you could still do it. Events are a great way to stay in front of your people. This could be a great way to meet new people too, but we will get into that a little later. Let's stick with our sphere here. Just like pop-bys, you have lots of opportunity for touches leading up to the event and after the event. Here are some ideas on events you could host.

- Customer Appreciation
- House Warming Party
- First Time Home Buyer Seminar
- Vendor Appreciation
- Easter Egg Hunt
- Fundraiser Drives
- Back to School Drives

While putting on the events is really fun, it is also really important that you take the time to be human. These events could potentially get you more families to serve, but if that is what this is about for you, then reconsider your approach. The point here is to build and maintain genuine relationships. You cannot trick people into coming to an event so you can shove your hidden agenda in their faces.

Handwritten Notes

Of all the touches we've discussed, handwritten notes are one of the most forgotten approaches. Let me ask you this, when was the last time you received a handwritten note in the mail? When you received it, how did it make you feel? Do you still have it? I love receiving cards and I keep every single one of mine. I find that when I share this with others, they often feel the same too. So what are we sending cards for? Here are a few examples for you:

- Birthdays
- Various Holidays
- Mother's Day/Father's Day
- Thinking of You
- House-Aversary's
- Thank You
- Sympathy
- Just Because

There's one thing I haven't mentioned that I want to make very clear: sending out "farming" pieces is not the same as sending someone a handwritten note. The objectives are different. Could you send people monthly or quarterly updates? Of course. It isn't part of this strategy though. This approach is another way to let people know that you care and you are thinking of them. It shows them that when working with you, it isn't just about the transaction. It is so much more than that.

As we wrap up the different ways you could stay top of mind with your database, it is now time to create *your* plan. Below is an example of how you can create an intentional plan. In the resource section of this book you will find where to go for the full fillable version. For now I want you to focus on this one part.

SOI: Sphere of Influence

What are you going to do to nurture your sphere? How many deals to you expect to receive from this group? How many did you receive last year?

Add the WHAT/THE PLAN below:
- I intend on _____
- I intend on _____
- I intend on _____
- I intend on _____
- I intend on _____

Now, add the # of deals you intend on gaining from this strategy & multiply that by your average sales price.

Enter Total --->

Once you have completed this section, the last thing I want you to do is look at your plan and think about how many families you could help if you leaned on this core group. If you were to fully execute everything you created, how many families could you help that have a real estate need? Then, I want you to take that number and multiply it by your average sales price. If you don't know your average sales price, then you can either use your brokerage's numbers or look in the MLS and look at your area's data.

Let's take a brief timeout and zoom-in on a special point. I know I just spent a lot of time going over how to be human and relational with the people in your database, and then here I go closing this out with talking about business. Just in case this thought came into your mind, I want to discuss it. I stand behind everything I've shared. I believe in my core that showing up and being you without being annoying about what you do, can in fact feed your business beautifully. Isn't that why we are here in the first place? The fact of the matter is, numbers in our business matter. We have to face it head on.

Lead Generation Strategy #2

While the first strategy was focused on your Sphere, this second and third strategy are going to depend upon you. A sphere is a sphere, and everyone has one. How you decide to show up in other ways, as far as lead generation goes, should be based around your strengths, what's in your wheelhouse, and where you are right now in your life. Something else that is just as important when considering which direction to go in is to think about what makes you happy. Real estate is already stressful enough, so we may as well have some fun while we're at it. To be honest, if you can't find joy in what we get to do, you are probably doing something wrong.

For your next strategy in this section, we are going to focus on getting you in front of people who have expressed in some way that they have a real estate need. What the heck am I talking about? Let's get to it. Here are some examples of different approaches that you could incorporate as a second strategy:

- Open Houses
- Hosting Seminars (Buyer/Seller/Investor)
- For Sale By Owners (FSBO's)
- Expired Listings

Since each of these will require a different approach, let's break them down one by one.

Open Houses

Open houses can be a lucrative way to build your business. Whether you are new or seasoned, everyone can host these and find success. As I mentioned earlier, this is one of the ways I got started when I got into real estate. One, because they were relatively easy; and two, I took a year off before getting into real estate since I had limited funds to work with—this was a no brainer.

Now, open houses may be an easier strategy but it's more than just putting a sign in a yard. It requires intention and preparation. Intention specifically around what you are looking for.

- Are you looking for sellers?
- Are you looking for buyers?
- Are you looking to get exposure?
- Are you hoping to sell the house you're holding open?
- Are you looking to book appointments from the open house?

I know those might seem like obvious questions but if you don't know what you're looking for, how will you know when you found it? How do you know how to prepare or what questions you should be asking? You study, study, and study some more.

You first want to learn everything you can about that home. I tend to focus on and really memorize the basics of the home and any upgrades or special features about it. This is of course if I am holding a home open on another agent's listing; if it is mine, I know all of that information. You then want to learn about the neighborhood, what other homes are active right now, and how many are pending. Then, you can ask yourself further questions, like:

- How many closed in the last 3-6 months?
- Are there any FSBOS's you need to know about?
- How do the sales compare to other neighborhoods or last year?
- What is close to the property?
- Are there any other houses similar to that one that are also for sale maybe close by?
- Do you have predetermined days and time available in case you have the opportunity to book an appointment?

The more prepared you can be the better, and speaking of which:

- What do you now prepare for at the house?
- Do you have anything printed? What are you printing?
- How about open house signs in sheets?
- Do you plan to have feedback forms ready for people to fill out? Will you have these available on paper or digitally?
- Are you going to walk the neighborhood? Will you walk the neighborhood before the open house or after?
- What will you say to the neighbors if they answer?

- If it's a new listing, will you hold it open for an hour before for just the neighbors?
- Are you serving food and/or beverages?

Something else to consider too is your signage:

- Are you allowed to put signs out in that neighborhood?
- If you can, how early can you put them out? When do you need to pick them up?
- Do you have signs? Do you have enough signs?
- What do your signs say? Are there dates and times on them? Do you have big flags or balloons to catch people's eyes?
- If you aren't allowed to put out signs, what's the plan to get people there?
- Will this be advertised online anywhere? On social media?

Once you get through gaining clarity around getting ready, you've got to find the house. I remember when I first started I would do any and all houses sent my way. I was very grateful, but most of the time they were duds—I would do all the prep and practice and nothing. I started to do a lot of research around these houses and found four elements that stand out above the rest: location, price, days on market (DOM), and *opening my eyes* to the neighborhood. Here is what I learned through my research and experience:

- Location: Where the house was located mattered. If it took someone more than four or five turns to get to the house they tend to lose interest. These were not my most successful opens.
- Price: The price of the home could play into this as well. I found holding regular open houses on homes ranging from $300k - $500k were great. Also, homes that were overpriced did not go well either.

- DOM: How long has it been on the market? I found the newer homes went a lot better than homes that had been on the market a lot longer.
- Opening my Eyes: The last thing I noticed was that when I walked the neighborhood I was more successful.

Taking the points I just shared, let's create what could be a plan for you to successfully host open houses. As a bonus, I will share how this could show up on your calendar.

1. Find the home on Monday—Tuesday, at the latest. (30 minutes)
2. By Wednesday, the marketing should be done and added to the MLS. (30 minutes)
3. On Thursday and Friday, you should be marketing the open house. (5 minutes/day)
4. Throughout the week, spend time doing your research and getting everything ready. (1-2 hours)
5. Walk the neighborhood. I was always taught the 10-10-20 rule. That means, you walk 10 homes to the right of the property, 20 across the street, and then 10 coming back the other way to the left of the property. Depending on the weather and the timing of the year this could be 5-5-10. (1 hour)
6. Hold the open house. (2-3 hours)

Total Investment of your Time: 5-7 hours per home each week.

Lastly, here are just a few more things to have prepped and ready to go before diving in:

1. Decide how many open houses you want to host each month—should NOT be every single weekend; you need a break and time off.

2. Have your follow up system ready to go to keep the conversations going, even after the open house.

3. Keep a spreadsheet, or better yet, a CRM to do this.

Hosting Seminars

Hosting seminars is another great way to meet people that want to buy or sell, but need guidance and/or more information. Each one of these serves a different purpose. What you will want to decide is if this is a strategy you are willing to commit to. Is this something you can do or want to do? I do find that these can be really successful because this strategy focuses on educating the clients, and when you can do that, in their eyes, you are the expert—that is a huge value! Let's break each one of these down.

Buyer Seminars

This type of seminar is probably the most popular one agents decide to go for. Why? It's because, when they start, most agents tend to work with more buyers than sellers. Not all of the time, but that is true for most. This is an easy way to get in front of several buyers in one place. Furthermore, these seminars serve to educate and show the value you bring as their real estate agent. I have been part of a few, and if done right, they could fill your pipeline really well. This approach may require you to have a little more patience, a sick follow up game, and have a solid team to help you help your buyers.

Now, before you go jumping in and throwing one of these tomorrow, you may want to slow down and create a before, during, and after seminar plan. Without it, you are wasting your time.

- <u>Step One:</u> Find a lender that can partner with you. Maybe that lender could sponsor lunch and you sponsor a give away from you, if you can afford to. When choosing a lender, make sure you are clear on what you are looking for from them. Having clear communication here can be huge. I also like for the lenders I work with to be solution oriented and creative.

- <u>Step Two:</u> Find buyers to invite to the seminar. You could start with asking people you may know. You could look for properties that have absentee owners—there is a good chance their home is a rental. You could send mailers to renters in apartments. You could even place an ad on social media to attract buyers. The point here is to be strategic and intentional.

- <u>Step Three:</u> Have a communication and touch plan in place before you start marketing for it. When someone signs up, how do you thank them? How do you send out timely reminders about the seminar? Are you texting, mailing, emailing, or posting about it? Maybe all of them?

- <u>Step Four:</u> Have a simple clear outline for the seminar. Remember that the potential buyers coming in are already feeling overwhelmed and nervous. No need to get into any weeds right now. Also, it is helpful to have something there for the buyers to take notes on.

- <u>Step Five:</u> What is the follow up plan behind the event? Some of the people that come to the event could be ready now or much later. How are you going to earn their business through your follow up after? This really needs to be spelled out and ready before you hit go. If not, even with the best intentions, you will drop the ball.

Every time I attend or host one of these events, business definitely picks up. Whether the improvement comes right away or later, I definitely add people to my pipeline. I generate quality conversations, all while continuing to add people to my pipeline for future business.

Seller Seminars

These aren't as common, but if you find that you are meeting homeowners who are on the fence on selling, and you know the market is good for them to sell, maybe organizing one of these can help them. Not everyone will want to sell still, but at least you shared with them their options. They could possibly reach out at a later time to sell.

That being said, what is the plan again for before, during, and after the seminar? Similar to the last one, here are some steps to help you.

Step One: Find a vendor(s) to partner with. You could have an inspector there to talk about preparing the home. They could share the value in a pre-list inspection depending on the age of the property. A lender could talk to them about options, too, especially if they would be selling and buying another home.

Step Two: Find sellers that could be next to sell. This step will require extensive research on different neighborhoods and each specific home. Things to factor in would be how long they've lived there, the turnover rate in the neighborhood, and how much equity they could have in the home they aren't aware of.

Step Three: How will you invite these folks to the seminar? Just like the buyer seminar, you need an intentional plan around your communication. You've got to get people there, keep them engaged, and then help them with a plan after the event.

Step Four: Have a simple clear outline for the seminar. You could have your seller's packet there, or to keep it super simple, provide them with FAQ's.

Step Five: What is the follow up plan behind the event? How will you lean on your other vendor partners to get them ready? Having this list could be really valuable for a seller. Heck, for you too.

I do find that it is a little harder to get sellers to one of these. If you establish a clear message and a "what's-in-it-for-them" approach, people may come. If they do, that could mean they are serious. Don't drop the ball!

Investor Seminars

I don't know how long you've been in the business, or if you have experienced this yet, but when I help someone purchase a home, I do like to talk to them about investing too. I have learned over the years the value in owning real estate, and I have seen how it can help a family build generational wealth. If you are someone who is an investor or works with them, this could be a great avenue for you. Maybe you can teach people how to do this because you have done it.

Just like the other two, you definitely want to have a clear picture of this person and a path to find them. This one could be really great as a mini series. And please, don't forget about the followup afterward—it is crucial.

* * *

For Sale By Owners aka FSBO's

Just like any of the other strategies we've spoken about, this one too takes some thought. Could you knock on a FSBO's door and just ask for the listing? Sure. Does that often work? No. Could you knock on their door and "say" you have a buyer? Sure, but do you? Listen, I am not mad at the guts it takes to go after FSBO's, but don't BS them. Unlike some of the other strategies, you know exactly why they choose to sell their home themselves—it is the biggest objection you'll face.

If you want to focus in this area, then you need to create a plan of what value you can offer them as their listing agent. This is going to take time and consistent effort. Once you create a list of "value" pieces, you have to figure out how you are going to roll them out. How many FSBO's will you try to keep track of at any given time? How often will you contact each one? Here are some ideas on what could be of value to a FSBO:

- You can offer them a Market Analysis each month
- You could supply them with open house sheets branded to you
- You could host an open house for them
- You could give them safety tips for when hosting their own open house
- You could supply a checklist

There is also nothing wrong with starting out previewing the home. Practice coming from a place of curiosity. If you are out there learning the market and each neighborhood, share that. If you can help it, don't lie about what your intentions are—people are going to smell that a mile away and you will not earn the business. The other thing you can do, aside from practicing the objections, is to create a list of questions you can ask them to learn about them and their home.

Expired Listings

Last but not least, expired listings. If you don't know what an expired listing is, allow me to explain. An expired property means someone tried selling their home with an agent, and it did not sell prior to the expiration date of the agreement. Why does this happen? It could be for a number of reasons:

- The price could have been off.
- The location or condition could also have been adverse.
- It could have been poor marketing, too.

I have seen expired listings work in two ways:

1. Going after an expired listing the day after it expires (like everyone else).
2. Going back a few months or a couple of years.

Both approaches work. In my experience, I do find going after an expired right away once it just expired takes a little more of an aggressive approach. What you need to figure out is how you will convert these sellers if they are still wanting to sell. *They tried selling it with another agent already*, so why you? What will you do differently? What value do you bring to the table with them?

Once you can figure out the value that you can bring to an expired listing, what's next? Similar to the For Sale by Owners, you need to figure out a few things.

- What tools do you need? What systems do you need in place?
- What is your message? What's your approach?
- How many properties are you going to go after at any given time?
- How will you stay in contact?
- How often will you communicate with this group of people?

Don't just go in blindly and wing it. Take the time to do the proper research. What happens if they are still thinking about selling but now isn't a good time anymore? How will you know how and when you will follow up? What other common problems do they all share? Aside from asking them questions, know what their objections are going to be. Learn.

Let's Close This Section Out

Well, look at you. You made it through the second section. What do you do now? You need to pick a strategy that aligns with you and one you can make a commitment to for the next ninety days, at minimum. Once you choose it, then you will want to decide what activities you choose to do on a daily, weekly, monthly, or quarterly basis.

When you have chosen your activities, then you want to get them on your calendar. If you aren't spending time putting this somewhere, even with the best intentions, you will not do it. I want to also add that as you start to create your plans and set your goals, creating your own schedule will feel a little weird. It is easy to follow directions from your boss. But now that you are your own boss, will you do what you said you would? What's it worth to you? Who will call you on your crap and hold you accountable?

I learned the hard way the difference between proactive and reactive ways of doing things. That, and finding someone who would keep me accountable. As counterintuitive as it felt, I noticed the stricter I got with my time, the better quality people I attracted. Turns out when I learned to get in front of my day, I had more of it to enjoy. I wasn't chasing my tail anymore trying to figure out where the heck each day went. I slowed down and started to look at not only monetary investments, but where I was spending my time. I could not believe how much time I was wasting when I started to pay attention.

Storytime

Oh my gosh! So, I have to share how the whole time blocking thing for me got started. It's funny to me now, but I hope it inspires you to build a business you are happy with and proud of. When I got into real estate, I knew nothing about it. I remember spending a lot of time writing and rewriting my bio. I made and remade buyer and seller books. I was only doing "busy" work. In the middle of it, I felt like I was accomplishing something but in reality I wasn't getting any business. My broker at that time challenged me to track how I spent my time for two weeks. She said to track everything from when I woke up til I went to bed. I thought, ok, I can do that.

Here is what I now find funny, I did not know what I did not know. I never used a planner before, let alone a time blocked planner. I went on a hunt for one that allowed me to time block by the hour. The only thing I could find was a damn salon book at Sallys. I bought it and turned it into what I needed... And it freaking worked! What I learned over those two weeks was that I wasn't really lead-generating. Aside from floor duty and the occasional open house, I wasn't getting business from anywhere else. I did some things that worked, but it was nowhere near what I needed to survive. The thing that changed the most for me was learning how to ask for the business. I was putting in the effort, but I kept expecting more from other people.

I really thought that if I just did a good job, or showed people I cared even an ounce, it would be reflected in my business consistently. That was not the case. Certainly, it was part of it, but there was something missing.

And in case you're wondering, I have since graduated to a proper planner for my business and life. :)

My next lead generation strategy is: _____
What are you going to do specifically to find buyers/sellers? How many deals to you expect to receive from this particular strategy? Did you get any from this strategy last year? How many?

Add the WHAT/THE PLAN below:
- I intend on _____
- I intend on _____
- I intend on _____
- I intend on _____
- I intend on _____

Now, add the # of deals you intend on gaining from this strategy & multiply that by your average sales price.

Enter Total --->

Just like you did after creating your plan around your sphere, I want you to look at your plan and think about how many families you could help if you did everything you just wrote. If you were to fully execute everything you created, how many families could you help that have a real estate need? Take that number and multiply it by your average sales price. If you don't know what your average sales price is, then you can use your brokerage's numbers or look in the MLS and look at your area's data.

Lead Generation Strategy #3

Last but not least, the final strategy. So far, we have worked on creating a plan or our sphere. We talked about working with people who have their hands right now with a potential real estate need. Now, we are going to talk about getting in front of new people. Meeting new people will give you an opportunity to build new relationships that could lead to business down the road. This is a great way to build a future pipeline. This strategy is going to require you to not only meet new people, but also have a plan of how you are going to keep it going too. Most new people you meet won't have a real estate need right away or know someone else that does. They don't even know you enough to trust you with a massive transaction yet. It will be your job to keep in touch and share your value with them over time. Keep in mind that you are going to be investing a bit of your time. You may also consider investing money, if you have the budget for it.

I am not a huge fan of recommending agents blowing all of this money at once. However, there is some truth in the phrase, "you need to spend money to make money." As you think about where you want to invest monetarily, consider these steps first:

- Set a budget per month.
- Create a list of the ways you could invest. List all of the strategies that come to mind.
- Go through each of those and pick the top three that align with you, that play into your strengths, and that fall within your budget.
- Do extensive research around each of those and create a plan of attack, a follow up plan, and what systems you'll need to execute each one.
- Map out the worst case and best case scenario for each option. In other words, how long will your investment last before you need to pull out or run through your money? How many closings do you need for this investment to be a win for you?
- Analyze all three options and decide which one is best for you. You should have a time deadline. I recommend giving yourself at least six months.
- Make a commitment, attach your why, and find an accountability partner.

Here are a few examples of what kind of lead strategies fall into this category:

- Networking
- Referral Group(s)

- Social Media
- Farming
- Online Leads

Networking

This is one of my favorite ways to find business. Not only do I always meet incredible people, I get quality business from them too. Oftentimes, when I am discussing this particular strategy with agents, I find that for many, they aren't quite sure what to do or say. Why, you wonder? It can be for many reasons. If you came into this business from a W2 job, you probably didn't have to do this, ever. If this is you, own that. If you want to learn how to get great at this, you can, even if you don't see it right now. This is going to push you out of your comfort zone—embrace it and push through. I can understand how for some it is much easier said than done, but you can do hard things. I believe in you.

Here are my best tips for successful networking:

1. Set your intentions for each event. What I mean by this is, know before you attend *who it is you are looking for*. Establish what would make this networking opportunity a success. Is it the amount of people you'd be talking to? Is it speaking with a given number of people? Or is it the amount of appointments you set? Maybe it is how many business cards you hand out?

2. Be prepared to share about your business, but don't lead into conversations that way. There is nothing less attractive than you going up to someone and shoving your business card in their face. That is the worst way to network and no one will ever call you.

3. When you are meeting people, come from a place of curiosity. Ask questions about them. Why did they come to that event?

What do they do? Why did they start their business? Who is their ideal client? If you are enjoying the person you are speaking with, you could ask if they would like to meet up for coffee or lunch.

4. Think about the questions I just listed before and *answer them*. Be ready to answer questions about your business. Even questions you wouldn't ask others directly, like: What is your elevator pitch? What value do you offer your clients? What's the experience like working with you?

5. This last tip is the most important one I've got to share on networking: have a darn follow up plan. To maximize your efforts you want to think about how you will stay connected to each person. Do you add them to your database? Do you call after an event? Do you send them a "nice-to-meet-you" card? Do you meet with each person one on one throughout the year? How do you know when to ask for business? What value do you add to their lives?

As it may appear, I have only shared investing your time right now. While there are plenty of ways you can do this for free or relatively cheap, you may do research around any events happening in town that do cost some money. Before I ever invest resources into one of those, I like to ask myself:

1. If I spend, *insert dollar amount*, what do I need to happen at this event for this to be a solid investment? What does a win look like, here?

2. Who do I want to meet at this event? I specifically think about people that are ahead of me in this industry. People that I can learn from.

3. Why do I want to go? Is this event aligned with the direction I am heading?

I know for some people this is extremely difficult to do. I really want to encourage you to push yourself a little bit. You have so much to offer to the world. Don't hide it and be a secret agent. Not only could this be a great way to build business, but the relationships you build could last a lifetime.

Referral Groups

This has been another factor that helped my business thrive. I am not going to lie, though; this might take a couple of tries. Similar to going to networking events, there are so many referral groups out there that you could potentially join. Some will be free and others will charge you. I have seen costs anywhere between fifty to a few hundred dollars a month. This is why knowing your budget can help you drill down which ones you can afford to join. Finding the right group that aligns with you is going to be the most important goal you are looking for.

Now, the whole point of joining one of these groups is to refer to each other's business. Just like when you start to network, no one really knows each other well just yet. One of the best ways of doing this I've found was meeting with one person in that group every week. Here is what I did when calling someone *in the group*.

1. I found a day and time that I would book these appointments for, and then made space for an hour each week.
2. I made a list of the people I would call.
3. I booked my month in advance.
4. I sent a reminder before that day, and I asked them to bring any marketing pieces they had to share.

5. I would then meet with the intention of learning about them, their family, and their business.
6. After we met, I sent a handwritten card saying "thank you."
7. I added them to my database and set reminders on my outreach to them.

Did you catch the *in the group* above? No referral group has every single industry in the group. Don't let that cap you on who you can meet. If you are looking to meet other local businesses or local business owners, here is the play you can run:

1. Identify the "who's" you need to find.
2. Once you make the list and identify the industry, start to research who you need to know. You could use social media to ask your audience, join neighborhood groups and see who people recommended there, and also look on Google or Yelp.
3. Then, after doing more research on them, call and set an appointment. Make sure you reference the great reviews you read and praise them for building a wonderful business. Be honest and upfront about your intentions on why you reached out to them.
4. Run the same follow up play as you would do with all of your partners.

As a reminder, I have found that when building a genuine relationship from the get go, I had a good chance of gaining business, supporting someone else's business, and I made some pretty cool friends.

Social Media

I am just going to be brutally honest here. If you are not on any social media platform and you do not get business from it, then you might want to do something more productive with your time. I do not mean to imply that social media is an infallible tool—it isn't. However, if using it for your business is currently more of a pain than something you know how to derive genuine growth from, move on until you really do want to make this a big focus.

Now that I got that out of the way. Let's really dive into this powerful tool. When I am in conversations with agents, my experience has been this:

1. Totally gets it and gets business from it. Not much personal use.
2. Always used it for personal and family only. Doesn't know how to expand from there.
3. Never uses it. Does not get any business from social media.

Then I get these comments and questions:

1. I want to grow on social media, but what do I say?
2. Should I have both a personal and a business page?
3. Do I post the same thing on every platform?
4. What platform do I use?
5. How often do I post?
6. How about paying for ads?

As you probably know, the list goes on. So what does this all mean? It means to pay attention to what is happening around you. It doesn't matter if you are on every platform or none at all. What you need to figure out is *why social media?* Is this something you genuinely want to grow in, or is it because of someone else? Just like any other commitments you make, this is also going to require you to make one.

If you are going to spend time posting and engaging with your audience, then create a plan that helps you show up on purpose. The name of the game here is *consistency*. Oh, and don't forget that just because social media is social media, it doesn't mean this will be something you get rich from right away. Could that happen? Sure, like anything can happen. That's fine and all, but you can't grow a business on luck. How you show up matters and who you show up for matters, too. If you need to, pull out the ideal client avatar you created.

Here some questions you want to ask yourself before you create your social media content plan:

- Who is your target audience?
- What platforms are you going to post on?
- How many times a week will you post?
- What are you going to share aside from business?
- Are you going to spend money on advertising on social media?
- If so, what is your monthly budget?
- What will your call to action be?
- How will you know this is a success and you should keep with this strategy?
- How many families would you like to serve using this tool?
- Will you also have business pages?
- Where are you sending people to?
- How will you showcase your value?
- What does your follow up look like?

Ok, ok. I'll give you a break, haha. Now seriously, I want you to think about all of those questions. Please do not take for granted what these different platforms can do for you if you set the right intentions. And DO THE WORK.

I am going to share one more thing that might ruffle some feathers. Looking at what you are using for lead generation, if social media is a "yes," let me ask you: how much closed business do you get? If the answer is zero, my friend, this is not a strategy for you. I am sorry if that stung, but for real, whatever you are going to invest time in, needs to bring you a return on that investment. Yes, it isn't money but time which is super valuable. It is the only thing that we do not get in abundance. Don't waste not even a minute. Make it count!

Farming

This is one strategy that I cannot stress to you enough: have a set budget, have a clear plan, know exactly how you will follow up including what systems you'll need, and have a year ready of time and money you can invest. I don't know what you have heard about this strategy, but it is still effective today if done correctly. I know of many agents using this strategy and are very successful. They are so successful because they have the right intention aligned with the right plan. The first thing you will want to know is how much money you have and if you can afford to give farming at least twelve months with no return. Then, you will need to spend time doing research around what neighborhoods you want to farm and why.

- Is it the neighborhood you currently live in?
- How many neighborhoods are you looking for?
- Are you looking for sellers and/or buyers?
- What needs to happen for this strategy to be a win for you?
- Be sure to include the plan for execution and the plan for when you get a "yes."
- The last thing to do is triple check one more time the best-case/worst-case scenarios before this is all good to go.

If you couldn't tell by now, I like to take a proactive approach to many things. The main reason being that if I don't do it this way, then I can guarantee that in the middle of actions with no visible results, my mind of negativity takes over. Doubts start rolling in, I start to say mean things about myself, and quitting becomes a possibility. I don't want that to be you. I want you to be so ready and so damn committed that nothing will stop you. You've got success rooted.

When I meet with agents who "farm", I often find that they farm an entire neighborhood. They send the same message to every single home. Why do you think my jaw drops every time I hear this? I'll tell you why. In my opinion, it shows the lack of professionalism and respect around hard work in this industry. Let me explain. A lot of agents say they don't farm because people just throw out their cards. What if we stopped right there and thought for a second why that could happen. What if the house you mailed your "scan here for your FREE home valuation" message just got bought and people have recently moved in? Would the card you just sent be of any value to them? Probably not. Could it be, over time? Sure. *That is why you want to conduct extensive research around the neighborhood.* To give yourself the best shot at seeing a financial return on the investment, you have to put your best foot forward. Don't waste time "testing" this. Do it right the first time and make it worth it. Now, I am not naive to the fact that, even if you send your cards out to the right people and with the right message, that they won't throw it away. If you keep sending the right message to the right people, they might actually start to keep those cards.

Most agents know about farming for sellers, but did you know that we can do the same with buyers too? Since there is a slight difference in the approach of connecting with buyers and sellers, I want to break this one down into two sections.

Farming for Sellers

Once you have made your decision and you've made the commitment that this is the way you want to go, let's walk through this step by step.

1. Create a list of neighborhoods you would be interested in farming. You should consider:

   - Turnover Rate
   - Property Values
   - Size of neighborhood

2. Conduct extensive research on each neighborhood:

   - Recent Sales
   - Sales History
   - Amenities/Upcoming Developments or Updates
   - How many potential sellers are there?
   - What would the cost be for each neighborhood? Does that fall into your budget?

3. Once you nail down the neighborhood(s), it is time to create the plan:

   - How are you going to market to them for "THE YEAR!"?
   - What is your CTA (call to action) going to be?
   - How are you going to follow up with your leads?
   - What systems or tools do you need for this to work?
   - Will you doorknock? Will you attend or host events as well?

4. Determine what you are offering as value. Here are some ideas:

   - Free Home Evaluations
   - Monthly/Quarterly Market Reports
   - Neighborhood Updates and/or Events Coming Up

Farming for Buyers

Let's say that you decided you want to put on a Buyer Seminar. How are you going to get butts on those seats? One of the approaches you take is farming. I really like this one because you can take on more areas and neighborhoods. You will find that there are far less renters in neighborhoods than there are people who own. This way you can sort of cast a wider net. The other thing you could do too, which will cost more, is farm to apartments looking for potential buyers. This isn't what I am necessarily talking about here, but it is an option.

When you are doing research around different neighborhoods, you want to look for absentee owners specifically. When I did this, I used a software my local mls provided, coupled with the property appraiser site. The beauty in this is that you now have two addresses: you have the home address for the people who are probably renting, and you also know where the people that own it live. These could be a wholly separate list of people you farm too. Here are some ideas of items of value you could send to a buyer in the scope of farming.

1. Renting vs. Homeownership Campaign
2. Home Buying Budget Guide/Planner
3. Invitation to a Buyer Seminar
4. Preferred Vendor List - Highlight your top 12
5. Market Trends/Education

As I wrap up this section, I did want to mention a few other ideas to enhance your farming efforts. Now, this might work best if you live in the neighborhood—the last thing we need is for anyone to look like a creep, ha! Here are some examples:

- Block parties around certain times of the year. You could tie it to a holiday too.

- Door to door with treats. You can also tie this to a holiday.
- Neighborhood Garage sales where you provide the signs (branded of course).
- Neighborhood Clean Up (You provide garbage bags and waters).
- Get involved with the association if applicable.

The goal is to get people to know you not only as a neighbor but a trusted source in the community as well. One last thing I will mention here is that you don't have to do this alone. Whether you are farming to find buyers and/or sellers, think about who you can partner with to do this. When you partner with a vendor or two, they may also help pay for the pieces you are sending out. That could help widen the net if you don't have a big budget. Don't be afraid to ask for help. There are lots of vendors out there waiting to help you.

Online Leads

Here we go. I saved this one for last because it is a popular choice for many. The biggest problem I see with this one is agents have the wrong expectations jumping onto this bandwagon. The misconception comes from people going into it thinking "I've got to spend money to make money." I do not one-hundred-percent disagree with that statement, but if you don't really have the money to invest AND do the follow up required, *don't do it.*

Online lead-in's are not another get-rich-quick gimmick either. These things take time and money to make them happen. Now, don't let me discourage you by what I just shared. I want to simply inform you and make you aware that you get to choose what you do. You are the only person that knows what you are actually going to do. The leads you get from this source are always going to be cold leads. You will have to work twice as hard to gain trust and build rapport with this group. That doesn't mean it can't be done, you just—say it with me now—*need a plan!*

Here are a few things to consider if this is something that is right up your alley.

- What online lead source are you going to use?
- Are you looking to partner with companies that charge fees upfront or when you close?
- If you choose to pay a monthly fee, how will you ensure you are working the crap out of those leads?
- What needs to happen for this to be a win for you? What will make it worth your while?
- What systems do you have in place to help you?
- If you create a solid plan, how many families can you expect/hope to serve this year?

Aside from paying for these third party online services, you can also purchase zip codes through Zillow, Realtor.com, Homes.com, etc. Everything I mentioned above still applies. There will be some people who swear by it but there will be more people who it doesn't work for. Why? There could be many reasons. What I want you to hear is that this will require WORK. Also, if you are going to commit and invest, then make it worth it. Invest the money and make it work for you at least four times. It is very easy to buy into one of these when you are down, but I often found that, for many, it was not worth the investment. To be honest, I think the fallout stems from a combination of the quality of the lead, the amount of leads to work with, and the lack of a long follow up game plan. Like I've already said, you are really going to have to put in the work.

One last thing I'll mention is that, since the leads come to you, it becomes a little harder to speculate about the outcome accurately. So it is going to be a numbers game. The more calls you make, the more leads you accept, the better off you and the quality of the leads get. You should always be studying the market, following up with other leads, and script practicing objections. Keep working and practicing on your conversations. This will help you convert more quality leads into real clients.

My next lead generation strategy is: _____

What are you going to do specifically to find buyers/sellers? How many deals to you expect to receive from this particular strategy? Did you get any from this strategy last year? How many?

Add the WHAT/THE PLAN below:
- I intend on _____
- I intend on _____
- I intend on _____
- I intend on _____
- I intend on _____

Now, add the # of deals you intend on gaining from this strategy & multiply that by your average sales price.

Enter Total --->

Follow Up

I am just going to say the thing that is going to sting when you hear it: if you are not going to follow up or if you think follow up isn't necessary, get out of the business now. I know that sounds brutal, but in all seriousness, follow up is just as important as lead generation. At least I think so. Why do I feel so strongly about this? I feel this way because the likelihood of someone you speak with about real estate needing assistance right now is low. Don't get me wrong, this could very well happen from time to time, but you will probably spend the majority of your time following up and keeping in contact until people are ready.

When I think of creating a plan for a follow up, I view it in three phases.

- Lead Generation Follow Up
- Under Contract Follow Up

- After the Close Follow Up

Looking at it this way, for me, helps create different systems, keeping it organized in my brain. Let's take a look at each one and create a plan around what each of these could look like for you.

Lead Generation Follow Up

Alright, so, creating a follow up system for this one could depend on what strategy you choose to focus on. That being said, you've got some options. As you pick up new leads you could put them in a daily week, long-contact system. That could be a combination of calls, texts, and emails. Then, transition them to something else depending on their response or lack of. You could follow up once a week with new leads. The choice is really yours. What I will suggest you don't do is to not follow up at all. I know that sounds obvious but hear me out. I am talking specifically when someone tells you that they are not going to be ready for a few months. What I have learned the hard way was to stay in contact with them anyway. Even if it's a monthly check in, do it. I remember in the beginning I thought I was being respectful by not "bothering" people until it was closer to the time they shared with me. Wanna know what happened? Yup, they bought or sold already with someone else. It crushed me every time. Who do you think I was mad at? At first, them—I won't lie, haha. When the dust settled, I realized I was the one who dropped the ball. I completely disappeared from their life and they forgot about me. I had no right to be upset at anyone else but myself.

The beauty in that lesson was that *I had the power to change that*. I had the power to create a plan that would keep me in front of the people I wanted to do business with. You can do this, too. The one thing I will highly recommend is having the right tool for this task. Tools like a CRM, a spreadsheet, a planner, etc. Please do not think that you can rely on your brain. Even with the best intentions, it is very easy to forget about people. Here is what you can do to keep your pipeline front and center, and most importantly, organized:

1. Organize your leads/pipeline into categories. Label them A, B, and C.

2. Define each category. This is how I defined them:

   A: HOT leads. These people are looking to buy and/or sell between now and three months at the latest. They may have something small to correct or fix. Follow up with this group every few days to at least once a week minimum. They are ready, willing, & able to move forward.

   B: WARM leads. These people are looking to buy and/or sell between three and six months. Follow up with this group biweekly. They are either ready and willing, but not able; willing and able, but not ready; or they could be able and ready, but for some reason not willing.

   C: Cold(ish) leads. These people are looking to buy and/or sell between six months to a year. Follow up with this group at least once a month, and please know that they are not ready, not willing, nor able to move forward. The primary focus here is to help them create a plan around how they will achieve whatever goal they share with you. They will for sure have something massive to work through and/or they are renting.

3. Add them to the right bucket and insert the right follow up plan for them. I do find it super helpful to ask a lot of questions up front to know not only their real estate needs but about them. That made it so much easier to stay connected. I had more to talk about and share aside from it always being about real estate.

You might be thinking, "Melissa, what about all of the other people I have in my database that don't necessarily fall into one of these categories? Do I just delete them?" Short answer: absolutely not! Unless someone tells you to screw off and never contact them again, stay connected. As you follow up and speak with others not on the pipeline list, take notes and add them to your system. Again, this gives you things to follow up on, and you can reference the last conversation you had the last time you spoke. You never know when someone can go from "not a lead," to "a lead," to "closed!!" Anything can change at any time in anyone's life. Be memorable.

Under Contract Follow Up

I like to talk about our system for communication when we are under contract separately because it is a big area of opportunity for real estate agents. There are two things happening or not happening when you, the agent, are under contract with your buyer or seller: you are for sure serving your existing client, or you may or may not be however lead-generating still— on that in a bit.

When you get your first deal or two, you will be excited and will probably over communicate to your clients. Maybe you have and you just laughed; I know, I am writing this. Now, I am not saying that over communication is bad; it is simply delivering more than you promised. That's how I like to look at it anyway. The problem comes when you have several of these leads you are juggling with, and you forget to update a client or you forget about important deadlines. You go from sharing a lot to not sharing at all. When people don't hear from us in a timely fashion, especially while under contract, they start to panic, and the last thing we need is for our clients to panic. That is why having a system around your communication will help keep things in order. Not only with what and where you need to be but also mentally. Using tools like a CRM, a planner, or a spreadsheet can help get these off your brain.

Once you have figured out your communication frequency and plan, you now need to share that expectation with your buyers and sellers. Here are a few questions to consider for yourself and your clients:

- What are my hours of operation?
- What am I willing to do?
- What am I not willing to do?
- What is your client's preferred method of contact?
- Where do you track when you need to follow up?
- What are you following up on?
- If you don't have any updates, will you still reach out?

Some of this may seem elementary, but I see this particular area as a common struggle with agents. I want you to be aware of this so you don't fall into the "24/7-agent" trap. It is not a fun place to be. If we are being honest, it is probably the opposite of what got you into this business in the first place. Don't forget it. I have witnessed this for myself. When I tightened up my calendar and got in front of it, I started picking up more quality people to work with. Respect yourself and the people that want to work with you will respect you too. It will work for you too.

The other problem I find happens is after all that work of lead generating that gets agents the business, a lot of them stop doing it, and all of their attention goes to service the business. The under contract follow up doesn't just stop when you are under contract. As difficult as this may seem, we do not have any other option. Unless you are cool with having a roller coaster career, then do you boo. I don't think that to be true though. The battle we truly face is finding time to do both. I believe that you will figure it out for yourself if it is something that is important to you. When there is a will, there's a way.

After the Close Follow Up

Well, you did it! You prospected for the right client. You found and/or sold their home and now closing is upon us. Once you finally close with a client, the relationship doesn't end there. It shouldn't anyways. If you want to be a relational agent versus a transactional one, you will want to listen up. If you are not sure which kind of agent you are, ask yourself this: Are you currently getting referrals from your past clients? If the answer is "no," then you may be a little more transactional than you might want to be. If the answer is "yes" you probably do a great job with keeping in touch.

I did share some ideas earlier when we were creating our touch-plan for our sphere. This is exactly what I am talking about you doing here too. You could have a campaign, and that is something everyone can receive from you. The others will be things interesting to that particular person or family. This is why having a CRM that you can plug these reminders and tasks into will be a huge lifesaver.

My hope for you is when you are doing this successfully your business will naturally transition to becoming more of a referral base business. In the beginning it's tough. You don't know what you are doing or who you are looking for. After a couple of years that can all change. Remember, people will do business with you when they know you genuinely care.

Wrap Up

As I wrap up this section, I really want you to know how important the piece we just discussed really is. This could be the one thing you are missing in your business. I have a few more thoughts I'd like to share with you to consider. One of the biggest complaints I get from agents is they don't know what to say or what could be "valuable" to someone. Here is where I want you to challenge yourself a bit. Deep down, I think you know what you could share as value to someone, but for some reason it escapes you. To help me organize my thoughts around this area, what I've done is breaking it down and writing it out. Have a huge brain dumping session of all the ideas you have. Let's take a look at a few examples I am referring to.

Items of Value for a Buyer

1. Vendor Partner List
2. Buyer Roadmap
3. Schools in the District
4. Sheriff Websites
5. Closing Checklist

Items of Value for a Seller

1. Vendor Partner List
2. Staging Tips
3. Kids Listing Agreement—*if applicable*
4. FSBO's in neighborhood
5. Monthly/Quarterly Market Update

Items of Value for Someone Relocating

1. Neighborhood Guide around home

2. Nearby Parks and/or Dog Parks
3. Vendor Partner List
4. Favorite Restaurants
5. Info on switching over their license

I find, it is easier to stay connected and keep the connections I've made at the top of my mind when I have other things to say or share with that person. Your follow up should not be just about real estate. The last thing I would like for you to take with you is this piece of information: if we are going to claim to be market experts, then we genuinely should be. Not only an expert on the market, but an expert in your community. Are you the source of information to people? If they need to know something, do they call you first to find out? That is a good sign because it means they look at you as a person of absolute value and care.

In the name of FOLLOW UP:

When do you intend on following up with your leads? How will you follow up with your leads. How will you keep it all organized?

I will follow up with my leads: _____
I will follow with them by: _____
_____
I will keep them organized by: _____
_____

What resources/systems will you need? _____
How will you stay accountable? _____

PART THREE

There are plenty of difficult obstacles in your path. Don't allow yourself to become one of them.

—Ralph Marston

Work/Life Balance

Let me start off by saying that there is no such thing as a perfect balance between your business and your personal life. That perception of having an equal amount of time for each is a load of crap. Balance for everyone is going to look a little different, so don't compare yourself to anyone else. When we start playing the comparison game, it's the quickest way to feel like a failure. It is never a valid comparison so don't do it. You might be wondering why? Well, let's take a look at the people we follow and "watch" on various social media platforms. Most people, even when they are trying to stay as true as possible, fall into the highlight reel of life. Oftentimes, what we are seeing from others are all of the great things happening and not enough of the true struggles behind the scenes. Now I know that there are things we don't want to share or shouldn't share, and that's ok. Remember that when you see someone only sharing the best of the best. That is not real life. I don't think it's a bad idea to be inspired by some of that, but don't put yourself down because you are comparing your insides to someone else's outsides. Sometimes the shit just ain't real.

What I can say through my experience is that work-life balance for me looks different every single week, even every month. It is why I have made it part of my life to look at each week/month and plan it out. It helps me to get in front of where I am spending my time. When I didn't do that, not only did I work more than I spent time with my family, but I was doing more busy work than anything productive. Want to know where that lead me? I had mom guilt big time, and no freaking business to show for it. Both my work and my family were getting less of what they deserved. To add, I not only fell into the trap of putting myself last; I was burning out fast. Truth? I don't have some magic science or percentages of how much time I spend on both sides. However, a few years ago I did come up with a way to make sure I gave me, my family, and my business the attention each one needs.

The first thing I did was create categories of what was important. They were things that I knew needed to be done every single week. I call these my "buckets." This was the best way I knew how to do that.

1. Me Time
2. Family Time
3. Lead Generation
4. Customer Retention
5. Administrative Work
6. Personal/Professional Development

Once I had that figured out, I started to add the "tasks/activities" under each one. Why did I do that? Well, let me ask you this. When you time block for, let's say, lead generation: what are you actually doing during that time blocked session? When you block this time on your calendar and just write lead gen or social media, how effective are you? I found it super helpful to be very specific on what that looked like. That saved me from wasting half that time on thinking about what I was going to do. Here are a few examples of what these buckets consisted of.

Me Time

- Working Out
- Puzzles
- Massage
- Quiet Time
- Meditation
- Anything that fills YOUR bucket

Family Time

- Game Night
- Extracurricular Activities
- Events
- Birthdays
- Holidays

Lead Generation

- Social Media
- Cold Calling
- FSBO's
- Expired Listings
- Networking
- Open Houses

Customer Retention

- Newsletters to Database
- Follow Up
- Listing Appointments
- Showing Appointments
- Consultations
- Open Houses

Administrative Work

- Data Entry (New Customers)
- Scheduling Showings
- CMA's
- Checking Emails
- Setting Up Systems
- Writing Offers

Personal Development

- Training/Classes
- Reading
- Coaching
- Seminars

This may look a little different for you and that's ok. Please, make sure that when you work on yours and stay true to who you are. Make time for the things that matter most to you. Then, the last thing you want to do is add these to your calendar. Whether you use a paper calendar or a digital version, you need to use one or both. I am a paper person, so I use a paper planner. The other thing I did was use a color coding system for each bucket. Each bucket (category) was assigned a color. That was important for me because I didn't want to spend a ton of time looking and reading through each and every day each time I reflected. By using this color coding system, that allowed me to quickly look at where I spent my time that week based on the colors that popped out at me. Again, I share this to encourage you to find the way that is going to work best for you.

Since we are on the topic of work/life balance, I want to be clear about something. If you are a new agent reading this, please understand that your work life lever might be a little heavier on the work side. It needs to be—at least for a little while. You are building a new business. It's ok to set proper boundaries so you don't burn out, but you can't expect to get what you don't put in. That's why you want to be crystal clear around your lead generation efforts. Learn to use your time wisely. As time goes on, it gets better. It gets better because you get better, thus giving you the opportunity to free up more time. One way of doing this could be focusing on your strengths and not working on your weaknesses. The weaknesses, you can learn to leverage over time. The things you are great at will give you the boost you need to find the right tools, systems, and/or people to delegate to.

Here is something else I really want you to think about. Out of any strategy available one can employ to build a business, the seemingly most hated one I get all the time is "cold calling." Many agents I talk to think this is still THE way to do it. While it might be a classic that yields results, it sure as hell isn't the only way. Now, why am I bringing this up? I am bringing this up because, I think it's safe to assume that you didn't leave a W2, steady paying job to build a business you hate. I don't care what anyone says, if you wake up in the morning and you aren't excited for what you are doing then you, my friend, are doing it all wrong. I want you to focus on doing things you enjoy doing. Do things that make you happy. Happy people are drawn to other happy people. You can't fake good energy—just saying!

If you are reading this and you are an agent that has been in the business for a few years, my questions for you would be:

1. Where are you spending the majority of your time?
2. Are they bringing you the ROI needed for the investment?
3. What are you doing that someone else can do?
4. Are you working from a calendar?
5. Do you take pride in being a 24/7 agent?
6. If I were to look at your calendar, would I hire you?
7. *Would you hire yourself?*

I know some of these are a little harsh, but man oh man, if you don't slow down every once in a while, you will miss everything that matters. You will miss life and what this is all supposed to be about. I'm going to say it again. If these questions hurt your feelings and you don't like it, you are ONE decision away from changing it. Do you want it bad enough? Only your actions will answer that one for you. You can do it!! I believe in you.

I want to circle back to what I said when I started this section. There is no such thing as a perfect balance. To those that know me, know I say this all the time: we are in the service business and because of that, I believe that *we are our business and our business is us.* I don't know how to live a life and work and keep them separate. I tried for a long time and it was the most exhausting, stressful time in my life. That's why for me, having boundaries helps keep me organized. Not just in my actions but in my thoughts too.

If you are a newer agent reading this and want to avoid burnout, then I encourage you to work from a calendar NOW. Take care of yourself. Without you, there is no business. There is no legacy. Is that why you got into this business? I don't think so. Do we or our families deserve less than they/we should be receiving? Absolutely not. Take some time and think about what matters to you most. Why are you here? How can this industry help you achieve more than you could have ever imagined? If you scaled back and got hyper focused on what truly matters, what would your world look like then?

Beautiful, isn't it?

If you are reading this and are in the midst of a burnout, please take a break. I am not talking about a few hours. I am talking about a few days. Go somewhere you can unplug from the world. Your body, mind, and soul are screaming for it. This will allow you the time to think and reflect on life.

Storytime

In August 2023, my hubby and I moved our family to Colorado. We are originally from New Jersey, but we moved to Florida and had been living there for ten years before moving out West. Everything I have shared thus far about boundaries and time has been something I've been working through and learning over the years. Prior to moving to Colorado, I had earned a lot of my boundaries and felt really good about where I was in my business. Then, my hubby got a job offer we could not say no to, so we moved. I don't know if you've ever experienced this before, but I was super excited for this because, at that time, my hubby had not worked at a place that appreciated him for a long time. Based on what we had learned about this new company, it was clear that they valued him and their other employees very much. They value and understand family first; then, work. While I was ready for the change, for me it meant I was starting all over again. With that in mind, I created a "plan." A plan that consisted of moving forward really fast, and taking very little breathers. The problem with that plan was I eventually hit a wall and hit it hard. I burned myself out. Now, I don't regret the way I went about building and starting somewhere new. However, after about a year, I needed a break desperately.

Labor Day weekend we planned on going off the grid. My hubby, the kids, and I went on our first tent camping trip. Not only was I excited for the trip because we have never gone tent camping before, but also because I was going to get a real break. That was something I had not done or honored for more than a year. Don't get me wrong, I would take breaks of course, but it wasn't often that I unplugged from work emails and social media fully. If you are anything like me, you can understand how hard it is to shut the brain off. Leading up to that weekend, I worked even harder on wrapping up all loose ends. I prepped emails, updated my calendar, cleaned, and let those that needed to know I was going to be unreachable for four days. Sidenote, for safety, I never post about when we are away—I only share about it when we return. Back to the story, I was so ready that as soon as we pulled out of the driveway, I shut off. It felt so damn good!!

If I can share something with you, as much as I was prepping and getting ready, I was secretly worried that I wouldn't be able to mentally unplug. I thought that I would be present with my family but not *present*. I shared with my family my intent and promise to them about not working, even in my head. You want to know something? I might have wondered in my head about work once or twice, but I actively shut it down. Nothing I would think about was even remotely as important as where I was at that moment. It was like I switched the off button and that was that. We had the most incredible time together. I am so grateful for it and it was a trip that none of us would forget.

When we returned, I felt refreshed and I felt like I had this renewed energy. I said to myself "it's time to start saying 'no,' Melissa." Here are a few questions I asked myself:

1. Why are you here?
2. Where are you heading?
3. What are you still aligned to?
4. What project can get moved back for now?
5. Are you done trying to prove yourself?
6. Who do you want to work with?
7. Who can help you close some gaps?

I took time to reflect on a lot. I made some decisions and some much needed changes. I gained great energy around prepping my next move. My biggest takeaway was remembering that I had the power to make the changes I needed to make. There was no need to beg for business. The people that saw value in me didn't question it. That felt really good. Also, nowhere did it say I had to work with people who didn't care about me or what I brought to the table. So there's that!

I share this story with you in hopes that if you are feeling like where I was, it's time for a break. It's time to stop, pause, and reflect on life. The people that care about you, love you, and value you will understand the changes you need to make for yourself.

Why does all of this even matter? It matters because you matter. It matters because why you got into this business matters. It matters because the people out there waiting for you matter. You don't have to sacrifice your family or your business. I believe you can find a way to have both. Do you believe it?

As I close out this section, I want to remind you of a few things. Ya know, in case someone hasn't told you in a while.

- You are perfectly imperfect
- You are enough
- You deserve the absolute best in life
- You have everything you need inside you right now
- You can do hard things

Know now that the journey you are on is super special and unique to you. Embrace it, it's yours. Oh, and don't forget to have a little fun along the way!

PART FOUR

The adventure of life is to learn. The purpose of life is to grow. The nature of life is to change. The challenge of life is to overcome. The essence of life is to care. The opportunity of life is to serve. The secret of life is to dare. The spice of life is to befriend. The beauty of life is to give.

—William Arthur Ward

Friends, if you have made it this far, allow me to offer you a high freaking five!! What you have just read and worked through isn't the easiest thing to do, but you did it!! I hope by now you understand the value of having a plan that is simple and also authentic to you. Before leaving you, I had a few more stories to share. As well as some other tips and resources I have picked up along the way. Throughout this book, I have shared a ton already about the many mistakes I have made over the years. Know now that you will still make your own mistakes too. My hope for you is that sharing mine gives you the confidence to keep going. None of us are perfect; we never will be. All of us have made mistakes and will continue to make them. If that isn't happening, then you simply aren't working. The one thing I want you to remember in all of this is that *your mistakes do not define you*. Take those lessons and turn them into something great.

In the final section of this book, I have three more lessons I've learned that have created the biggest impact in my life. Earlier in the book, I talked briefly about your transferable skills. The first story I want to share with you is around this topic. Prior to getting into real estate, I used to work in HR for a few years and I was also an Assistant Store Manager at a retail store. There were many things I was good at, especially organizing and paperwork. Why does this matter? It matters because this is something that by nature I am really good at. I actually enjoy it. You may know by now that there is a lot of paperwork and organizing when it comes to real estate transactions. Not only are we writing contracts, addendums, emails, etc, but we are also keeping track of the entire transaction. There are many hands involved with a real estate transaction and it is our job to keep them all organized. This may not seem like a big deal for some—and when you have a deal or two, it isn't. It is, however, when you are juggling five or more transactions at one given time. As good as I am at doing this, it is also not what I am solely being compensated for. It is also a ginormous time sucker.

I want you to take a moment and think about your business right now. In your head, do you see anyone else aside from yourself? If you don't, I want you to ask yourself the following questions:

1. Am I building a business big enough for other people's dreams to come true?
2. If I were to look at my business 5, or10 years from now, who is standing by me?
3. How big do I want my business or organization to become?
4. Who am I going to need to help me get to where I want to go?
5. What immediate thoughts come to mind while reading/ answering these questions?
   a. Are they positive thoughts?
   b. Are they limiting thoughts?

This started to become something I needed to change when I started losing clients because I was stuck elbow deep into some of this. To be honest, I was being a bit of a control freak too. The combo was deadly and not productive at all. It was a hard lesson to learn because through this, I was not only losing clients but once all of my deals had closed, I had nothing behind it coming up. I lost all the momentum I built. It was awful and the roller coaster career I didn't want. If you struggle with this, I want you to answer these following questions.

1. How much time do I spend on my listings?
2. How much time do I spend on my buyers?
3. If I were to add all of the hours I worked into my average GCI(Gross Commission Income), how much money does it say that you are worth per hour?

This is a tough yet enlightening exercise to do. If you are worth more than one hundred dollars, heck five hundred dollars an hour, why are you making booklets and tracking deadlines? All of which, I know, are necessary, but it doesn't have to be you. The most common first hire for a real estate agent is a transaction coordinator. They are part of your team and can help immensely with contract to close work. They can also help you with listings, too.

One last thing I want to share with you. When you get to a place in your business that you need the help but are scared, I want you to challenge yourself around why. Is there a mindset shift that needs to happen in order for you to open up to all of the wonderful opportunities waiting for you? Challenge what it is that you are so afraid of. Then, take ACTION! You got this!!

My next lesson to share with you comes with a funny story. I give you permission right now to laugh!! Going back to my early days in my real estate career, I had no idea about time blocking. I didn't know I was supposed to do that, and when I found out I should be, I didn't know where to begin. It was for sure a foreign concept to me. One day, I was meeting with my broker and I was expressing my frustration with my lack of results. She asked me what I had been doing. I immediately blurted out all of these things along with my being in the office 3 days a week. She gave me a puzzled look. Then she proceeded to ask me where my calendar was. I shamefully said, what calendar?

This is when she tasked me with the first major challenge of my career. She told me to get a planner and track everything I did for two weeks. I was to track everything I did from the moment I woke up until the moment I went to bed. On top of that, I was to track the amount of time I spent on each thing. I was eager for the challenge. I left her office and was on the hunt for a planner. One that specifically could track by the hour. As I went from store to store, I was not having much luck. Then, I went into Sally's. I don't remember what possessed me to go there, but I did. To my surprise I found a Salon Appointment Book. It wasn't perfect, but it did have hour by hour blocks that I could track my time. I went home and turned that book into my planner. I added dates and slots to add everything to it. I was to begin the very next day.

What I find hysterical now is I didn't know that actual planners like what I was looking for existed. I was so new and naive to this whole thing. All I knew was I was given a challenge and I decided I was going to find a way to complete it; I have always been a person of action. Fast forward two weeks, it was time to meet with my broker. I walked in excited to discuss with her what I had done. She quickly noticed that while I did good with tracking my activities, I was doing no lead-dollar-producing activities.

The clarity I found that day was the first major pivot I made in my career. I know sometimes it's hard facing the truth. Sometimes it takes being tired of our own shit to face it. I don't know where you are in this story, but you need to know this: if you aren't where you want to be, then it is time to face yourself. You are meant for so much more. Do not allow yourself to stand in your own way. One piece of advice I was given years ago that made me open my eyes was "you are only one decision away from creating a life you desire." Gut punch, right!?! You may not have all of the answers right now, and that is ok. Try focusing on one step at a time. The more steps you take, the more of your path you will start to see.

My last story is a juicy one. This was the area in my life where I needed the most help and didn't know it. I am taking a huge risk sharing this with you. It is quite a vulnerable story, but I trust my readers. I believe the more I share this, the more people this will help. It is so much bigger than me. Here we go...

As I mentioned in the beginning of the book, I got my first license in 2016. Even though I wasn't making a ton of money early on, I was still really excited when I got my 1099's. That money was money I made on my own. I was incredibly proud. What I wasn't proud of though was the lack of money I had in my bank account. Each year, I shared with my hubby what I made. He would also share his excitement and then he would ask me how much I had in the bank. I would flounder answering this question. The truth was I didn't have much in the bank. I could not tell him where that money went. I was embarrassed and really upset. Once I took my head out of my ass and stopped taking his question as a negative, I realized not only was he right but his question was legit.

I had never been bad with money before, so what was I doing? Where did it all go? That was when I realized I had a bad relationship with money. What was I to do? It was 2020 and I was having my worst year ever. I knew that the conversation we had every year was coming and I didn't want to have it. What I didn't want least of all, though, was a failed relationship because of money. I knew I had what it took to figure this thing out. Not only for my family's sake, but for me. I have big dreams. I will never achieve those if I don't fix this. Lucky for me, around that time a few friends of mine were reading this book called, Profit First by Mike Michalowicz. I told my hubby I was going to read it and I asked him to give me the whole next year to run the play.

That book changed my life. Because of what I learned in that book and the discipline I had around executing it, I achieved something I never did or thought I could do. I hoped and prayed but deep down thought "nope, not me." Not only did I have the best year I ever had at that time in real estate, I also could not wait to have that talk with my hubby. That year, I was able to pay off all of my debt, I saved a lot of money and I had over $12k in my account to pay for taxes the next year. *I had learned how to budget.* I learned how to make better decisions when it came to investing my money, too. I highly recommend this book to everyone who owns a small business.

This was also huge for me because I am not like most of my family members. That might sound negative or harsh, but don't take that the wrong way. There is nothing negative about that statement. What I mean is, as a child I always dreamed of owning my own business. I didn't want to work for anyone else. Growing up, I saw what that was like for my family. I wanted to build something that took care of people. A place where people could work for a long time with me or be so inspired through their experience at my company that they opened up their own business too. I didn't grow up knowing or having someone showing me the ropes. I had no one teaching me about business; I was born an entrepreneur. That is what I mean about being different from my family. I am learning everything the hard way. That is why I wanted to write this book. I may not have all of the answers or solutions for some of the mistakes you might make on your journey, but I sure hope this cuts down your curve. I want you to be more successful and much faster than me.

Recap and Takeaways

As we near the end of our time together in this book, I can only hope that this has given you some clarity and direction around your life and business. I want to take this opportunity to recap everything you just learned throughout this book. I realize there has been a ton covered and you might still be trying to figure out how to pull this all together.

For starters, what is your income goal? This is something you will need to know before jumping into any kind of plan for your business. Knowing your financial goal for each year will help you stay grounded and disciplined, each and every day. What you also might want to spend some time thinking about is how much income do you want to keep. Many agents in the beginning will make a gross income goal of one hundred thousand dollars. That isn't bad, totally doable even being new. But out of that money, how much do you want to keep? How much of that is going to be profit for you? As you start to make some real money, you will naturally transition to creating income goals around your net versus gross income. So, let's say you now want to net one hundred thousand dollars. If that's the case, you will have to gross more than that amount.

Then, the next step will be to figure out the math going backwards from your financial goal. Below is a simple math problem to help you do just that. Ultimately, what I want you to learn is how many families you will serve that following year. This is often discussed as units. I like to focus on the families because it makes what we do more relational than transactional. Plus, when you are sharing your goals and asking for support, it rolls off the tongue better too. Let's take a look at an example.

Sales Unit Goal Example

Income goal = X
Average Commission per sale in your market or your own average
Average Sales Price x commission % =
X * % (commission split) = average commission per year
Income Goal/Average Commission per sale = sales unit goal
Write down your goal: #

As you can see, in order for this person to hit their gross goal of sixty thousand dollars, they need to help 13 families at their average price point and average commission. I want you to take a few minutes and work *your* math out. How many families do you want to serve in a given year? Depending on when you are reading this, you are either planning for the next year or you might be considering a pivot in the current year. Either way, this is where you are going to begin. Once you gain clarity here, then you are free to start building out the *how* part of accomplishing this goal.

I spent a good chunk of time going into great detail around the how part of our jobs. It may have been a little overwhelming. Hopefully as you were reading, you were making note of what you could potentially build your business around. That being said, let's go back to your sphere. What ideas did you take note of? Were you able to complete that section? If not, go back and decide how you want to stay in front of and top of mind with that group of people. In the back of the book, I have additional resources for you to download. One of them is going to be this plan I broke down throughout the book. It is important to have all of what we've discussed in one place.

Now I want you to go back to both Section One and Section Two. What other lead generation ideas did you choose to build a business around? If you haven't chosen one yet, my friends, do it now! Don't worry about having all of the answers either. If you are new to this industry, you might find yourself trying a few different methods. I usually see agents by year two really start to find themselves. They discover what has worked and what they have done that also makes them happy. This is their authenticity coming out. Like I mentioned before, you will be told many ways you should do this. The only way is your way. The way that best suits you, not someone else. That was a lesson I also learned the hard way.

The last major part is going to be planning out your follow up intentions as well. Remember earlier, when I shared how I look at follow up. There is follow up for your lead generation, then there is follow up for when you are under contract with your clients, and lastly, there is your follow up for after the closing and beyond. Each one needs its own plan. Following this, there are going to be two more pages that will allow you to:

1. Create a summary of your intentions for the year for your business

2. And there is also a page that will help you focus on building a plan for *you*. Yes, you. If you are no good, your business will eventually suffer for it. Without you there is no business. Make sure to make this a priority. Seriously.

The very, very last thing I want you to complete is how you are going to track your business, how and when you will work on the business, and if this is applicable, writing your Future You a letter about where you are in business and life right now. That is either going to be a supportive letter to you, or a kick your own ass letter. You get to decide. Now, if you are local to me, I would be happy to grab this from you and mail it to you when you would like to receive it. If you are not local to me, it might be great to ask a mentor or a coach to help with this.

A few words of wisdom to share with you as you start building your ladder.

1. Of all the things we receive in abundance, time is not one of them. Spend it wisely.

2. Your journey is your journey. Embrace all of it. The best *and* the worst parts of it.

3. When you feel like you aren't going anywhere, or are experiencing losses, that is good! That means that you are on the cusp of growth, and that is magical.

4. DO NOT GIVE UP! You are only a failure when you give up.

5. Find someone who can help keep you accountable.

My Final Thoughts

Friends, thank you so much for going on this ride with me. I cannot believe that I am here writing this to all of you. I remember when I had my children and I took a year off, I kept wondering what was in store for me next. I sat in my home most days and stared at my babies. I not only wanted to do something extraordinary for myself but for them too. I wanted them to know what was possible if they took a leap of faith on themselves. With all of that, I wasn't quite sure what that would be. However, I knew I didn't want to go back into retail management. I had this nagging feeling deep down inside that there was so much more for me.

One day, my hubby came home and I was sharing with him my yearn for more. He threw out the idea about getting into real estate. Where did that come from, you might be thinking? I just so happen to be obsessed with HGTV. I am so grateful he put that bug in my ear. The next day, I did some research around obtaining a real estate license. I found that it wasn't terribly expensive to get started. We were able to manage the schedule with classes too. Our children were one and two at the time. I was getting all the good signals to move forward with it. I signed up and shortly began in-person classes.

One thing I don't think many people know is that I knew nothing about real estate. My parents bought and sold but I wasn't really involved. I honestly wasn't really sure what it all meant. I found real estate school to be very overwhelming. I remember thinking I would never learn all of this. To my surprise, I did learn it. I not only passed my initial exam to get a license, but two years after that I went back to school to get my Broker's license.

Those first two years, though, were rather difficult. Because of my lack of knowledge, it took me a long time to learn the things I didn't know. I spent a good chunk of my first two years in different classes, learning non stop. It took me many mistakes to learn what I was supposed to be doing. I was that new agent that asked a million and some questions, I doubted my abilities, I questioned myself constantly. I remember listening to other agents talk and thought to myself "I will never be able to talk about the market like them." This is why this book is so special to me. I don't consider myself the one-stop shop for perfection in this business at all. I consider myself someone who came in an underdog, and was determined to find a way.

I wrote this book for those who get into this business with high hopes and expectations for massive success. I wrote this to inspire you to find your way. Building any business is hard but you chose real estate. Never forget why you chose it. I believe in you. I know that you will make it, simply because you made the investment in this book. Please use this book as an active, ebb & flow resource. This book will help keep you aligned to what matters most. It will keep you grounded and disciplined during your hardest days.

I will leave you with this, as much as I hear this about parenting: "*it takes a village.*" So much is true for owning a business. I have a long list of people who have helped me, encouraged me, and believed in me all the way, and I am not done yet. Find your village. Lean on your people. Ask for help. Believe in yourself. Reach for the Moon.

You can DO this! Let's F*cking Go!!

Follow me and download additional resources on

cruzcontrolresources.com

About the Author

Melissa Cruz is a multifaceted professional—mom, daughter, sister, spouse, realtor, coach, and author—dedicated to guiding others and positively impacting her community and the real estate industry. Licensed in real estate since 2016 and as a broker since 2018, she has earned accolades such as Associate with Highest Outgoing Referrals (NC Region, 2018), GRI Designation (2019), and 25 Under 40 Honoree (2020). A graduate of the Florida Realtors Leadership Academy (2022) and TLR Leadership & Academy (2023), Melissa continually strives for growth.

Her passion for coaching began in 2019, mentoring real estate agents, and she joined The Locker Room as a coach in 2021. Melissa has spoken at various national real estate events. As an author, she co-authored the international bestseller "EmpowerHER Story Anthology," published articles in Florida Realtor Magazine and Health & Wellness Magazine, and developed real estate professional development courses.

Melissa's dedication extends to volunteer work, including over four years on the Education Committee, serving as Secretary and Director on her local board, and contributing to the Diversity State Committee. She also serves at DMAR on the Industry Partner and Leadership Ac and the DMAR Gives Committee. Outside of work, Melissa enjoys t with her family, music, puzzles, hiking, and cooking—values that gui her in every aspect of her life.

LinkedIn: https://www.linkedin.com/in/mcruz19/

Facebook: https://www.facebook.com/cruzm19
Instagram: https://www.instagram.com/mcruz.19/